PRIMATES

MANDRILLS

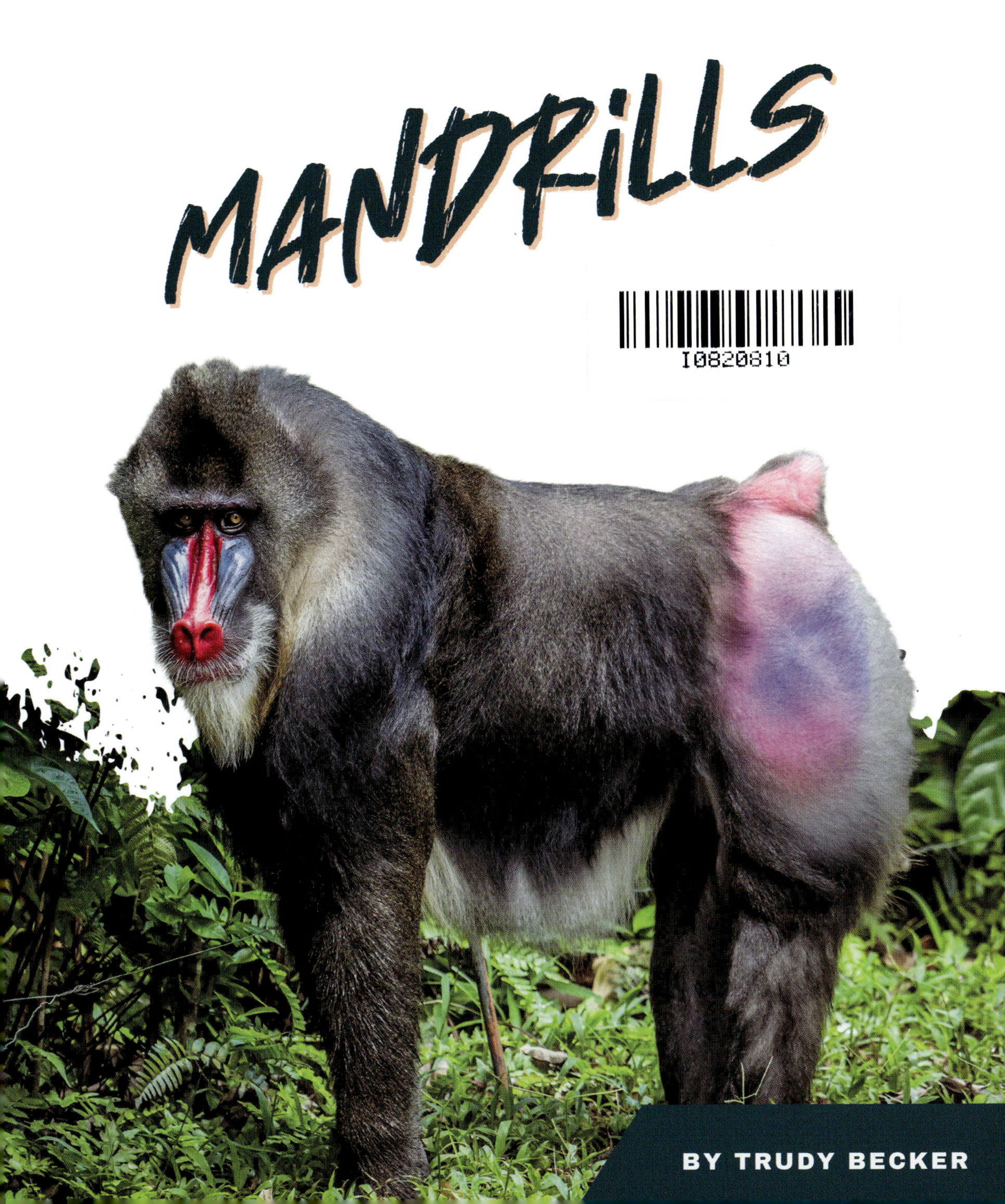

BY TRUDY BECKER

WWW.APEXEDITIONS.COM

Apex is distributed by North Star Editions:
sales@northstareditions.com | 888-417-0195

Produced for Apex by Red Line Editorial.

Photographs ©: Shutterstock Images, cover, 1, 4–5, 6, 12–13, 14–15, 16–17, 22–23, 24, 29; iStockphoto, 8–9, 25; Long Zhiyong/Moment/Getty Images, 10–11; Anup Shah/Stone/Getty Images, 18–19; Jorge Fernandez/Alamy, 20–21; Ger Bosma/Alamy, 27

Library of Congress Control Number: 2025939163

ISBN
979-8-89250-797-4 (hardcover)
979-8-89250-826-1 (paperback)
979-8-89250-882-7 (ebook pdf)
979-8-89250-855-1 (hosted ebook)

Printed in the United States of America
Mankato, MN
012026

NOTE TO PARENTS AND EDUCATORS

Apex books are designed to build literacy skills in striving readers. Exciting, high-interest content attracts and holds readers' attention. The text is carefully leveled to allow students to achieve success quickly. Additional features, such as bolded glossary words for difficult terms, help build comprehension.

CHAPTER 1

A CLOSE CALL

Several mandrills sit on the rainforest floor in Gabon. Some of the monkeys rest. Others play together. A leopard creeps toward the group.

Rainforests have warm weather and many trees. They get more than 70 inches (178 cm) of rain each year.

A male mandrill spots the leopard. The male barks and screams. Babies and females hear the loud sounds. They hurry up into the trees.

BABIES IN DANGER

Mandrills don't have many **predators**. But baby mandrills face the most danger. Leopards may try to catch them. So may eagles and pythons.

Male mandrills often watch over and protect females.

A mandrill's largest teeth can grow 2.5 inches (6.4 cm) long.

The leopard moves closer. But the male mandrill bares its sharp teeth. It jumps up and down. Finally, the leopard runs away. The mandrills are safe.

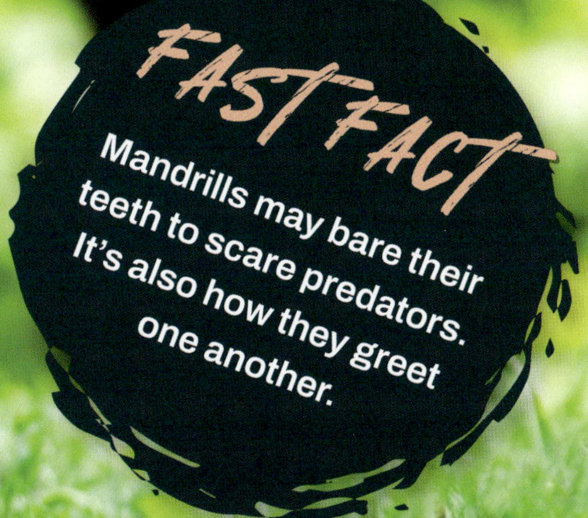

CHAPTER 2

ALL ABOUT MANDRILLS

Mandrills are **primates**. They are the largest type of monkey. Males can grow 3 feet (0.9 m) tall. And they can weigh more than 70 pounds (32 kg).

Male mandrills (right) are much larger than females.

Mandrills have very colorful faces. They have red noses with blue **ridges** along the sides. Some fur around a mandrill's face is gold. Mandrills have brightly colored backsides, too.

When male mandrills are excited, their backsides become more colorful.

Mandrills live near the **equator** in central Africa. Most make their homes in the rainforest. Some mandrills also live in mountain forests or **savannas**.

Many mandrills live in Gabon. This country is on Africa's west coast.

TROUBLE FOR MANDRILLS

Humans are damaging mandrill **habitats**. They cut down forests to set up farms or buildings. Some people also hunt mandrills for meat. So, the number of mandrills is decreasing.

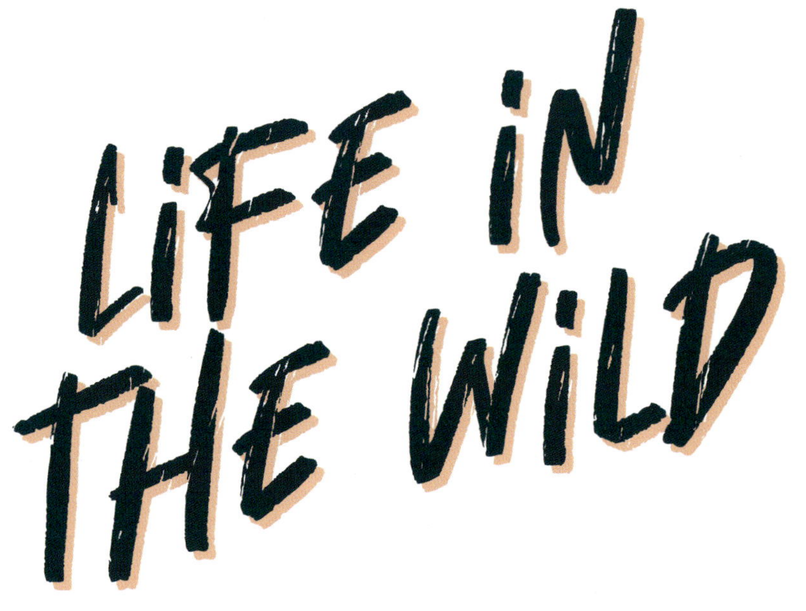

CHAPTER 3

LIFE IN THE WILD

Mandrills are **omnivores**. They eat lots of fruit. They also eat roots, insects, and **fungi**. They even eat frogs and snakes.

Mandrills often eat plant parts such as leaves and seeds.

Mandrills spend most of their time on the ground. At the end of the day, they climb up into trees. They sleep in the branches.

A mandrill finds a different tree to sleep in each night.

MOUTH POUCHES

Mandrills have deep pouches in their mouths. The pouches store extra food. They can hold about as much food as mandrills' stomachs.

Mandrills live in groups called hordes. Hordes can include hundreds of mandrills. Most members are females or young males.

Mandrills often travel and look for food in large groups.

CHAPTER 4

LIFE CYCLE

Males join hordes during **mating season**. Six months after mating, the females give birth. Each female usually has one baby at a time.

The dominant male in a horde mates with many females. He is often the strongest male.

A mandrill mother usually gives birth to one baby every two years.

Each mother feeds her baby milk for up to a year. At first, the baby clings tightly to her body. Over time, the baby learns to move and feed on its own.

CHANGING COLOR

A newborn mandrill's fur is black. Its face is pink. After two months, these colors begin to change. The mandrill grows gold fur and colorful skin on its face.

Females in a horde sometimes help raise one another's babies.

Female mandrills stay with their hordes for life. When males grow up, they leave. They spend most of their time alone. They find new hordes during mating season.

Female mandrills (right) are fully grown after about seven years. Males (left) take about nine years.

COMPREHENSION QUESTIONS

Write your answers on a separate piece of paper.

1. Write a few sentences explaining the main points of Chapter 2.
2. What fact about mandrills do you find most interesting? Why?
3. What color is a newborn mandrill's face?
   - A. gold
   - B. pink
   - C. blue
4. Why might baby mandrills face more danger than adult mandrills?
   - A. Baby mandrills are smaller and better at hiding.
   - B. Baby mandrills are weaker and easier to catch.
   - C. Baby mandrills move faster than adults do.

5. What does **damaging** mean in this book?

*Humans are **damaging** mandrill habitats. They cut down forests to set up farms or buildings.*

A. building up
B. making bigger
C. hurting

6. What does **decreasing** mean in this book?

*Some people also hunt mandrills for meat. So, the number of mandrills is **decreasing**.*

A. going up
B. staying the same
C. going down

Answer key on page 32.

GLOSSARY

equator
A made-up line that runs around the middle of Earth.

fungi
Living things, such as mushrooms, that break stuff down.

habitats
The places where animals normally live.

mating season
The time of year when animals form pairs and come together to have babies.

omnivores
Animals that eat both plants and animals.

predators
Animals that hunt and eat other animals.

primates
Animals in a group that includes apes and monkeys.

ridges
Raised strips or bumps that stick up.

savannas
Flat, grassy areas with few or no trees.

BOOKS

Kirkman, Marissa. *Gorillas*. Apex Editions, 2025.

Sommer, Nathan. *Mandrill vs. Chimpanzee*. Bellwether Media, 2025.

Wilson, Libby. *Mind-Boggling Mammals*. Apex Editions, 2024.

ONLINE RESOURCES

Visit **www.apexeditions.com** to find links and resources related to this title.

ABOUT THE AUTHOR

Trudy Becker lives in Minneapolis, Minnesota. She likes exploring new places and loves anything involving books.

INDEX

ANSWER KEY:
1. Answers will vary; 2. Answers will vary; 3. B; 4. B; 5. C; 6. C